# Modifying Your Site Navigation in SharePoint 2013

STEVEN MANN

## Modifying Your Site Navigation in SharePoint 2013

Copyright © 2014 by Steven Mann

### Trademarks

### Screenshots of Microsoft Products and Services

### Warning and Disclaimer

# Introduction

This guide steps users through the customization and modification of their site navigation. It is geared towards new users to SharePoint 2013 sites. The scenario in this guide involves a team site collection with multiple subsites and does not have the Publishing features enabled.

# Scenario

The scenario for this guide consists of a Team Site site collection that does not have publishing enabled.

The team site contains two subsites:

The subsites were created using the default selections and do not inherit navigation from the parent site collection.

## Top Link Bar - Edit in Place

The first thing to notice is that the top link bar contains the site collection link as well as the subsite links:

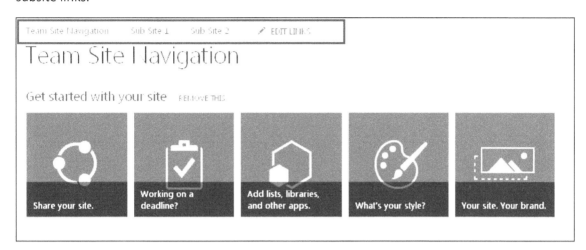

Right off the bat you may modify the links by clicking the EDIT LINKS button:

This places the Top Link bar into edit mode:

### *Removing a Link*

You may easily remove a link by clicking on the X next to it:

### *Reordering Links*

You may easily change the order by selecting a link and dragging it around the top bar:

## *Editing Links*

While the Top Link bar is in edit mode, if you click on the name of one of the links, you can quickly modify the text:

Enter new text and press the Enter key on the keyboard:

If you wish to edit both the display and the URL, click on the Edit Link button while editing the text:

The Edit Link dialog appears:

You may modify the Text to display and the Address of the link. Click OK when finished.

### *Adding a New Link*

To add a new link to the top link bar, click on the add link button:

The Add a link dialog appears:

Enter the Text that should be displayed for the link along with an Address. The address can be an internal SharePoint URL or any external web site:

Click OK.

The new link is added to the top link bar:

## *Saving Your Changes*

Once you have completed the top link bar modifications, click the Save button to save the changes and exit out of edit mode:

The changes are saved:

# Top Link Bar - Site Settings

You may also modify the Top Link Bar using the Site Settings. From the Settings menu, select Site settings:

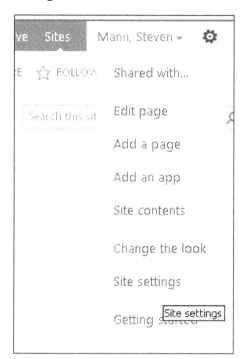

Under Look and Feel, click on the Top link bar link:

The Top Link Bar page appears:

Site Settings › Top Link Bar ⓘ

New Navigation Link | Change Order

- Team Site Navigation
- Site #1
- Sub Site 2
- My Blog

## *Removing a Link*

To remove a link, click on the Edit button next to the link you wish to delete:

The Edit Navigation Link page appears.

Click on the Delete button to remove the link:

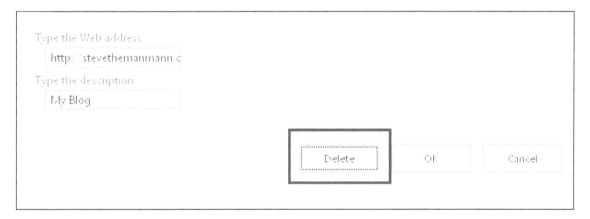

A confirmation message appears:

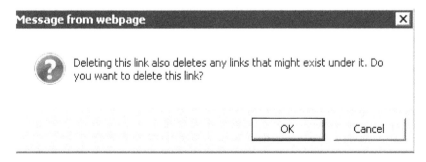

Click OK.

The link is removed:

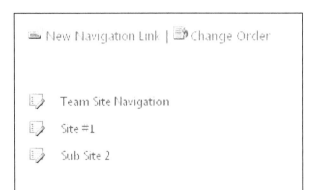

## *Reordering Links*

To change the order of the links click on the Change Order button:

The Change Order page appears:

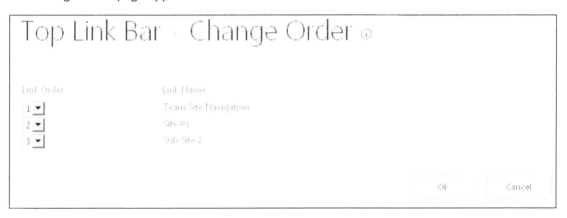

Use the Link Order buttons to change the order of the links:

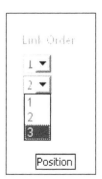

The links are reordered in place:

Click OK to save the ordering changes:

The new order is applied:

## *Editing Links*

To edit an existing link, click on the Edit icon next to the link you wish to modify:

The Edit Navigation Link page appears:

Here you may only modify the description:

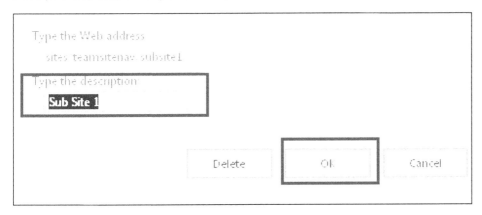

Click OK.

The modification is saved:

New Navigation Link | Change Order

Team Site Navigation

Sub Site 2

Sub Site 1

## *Adding a New Link*

To add a new link click on the New Navigation Link button:

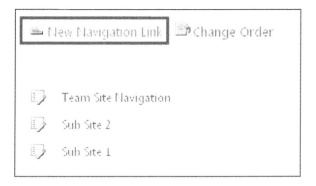

The New Navigation Link page appears:

Enter an internal or external web address along with the description:

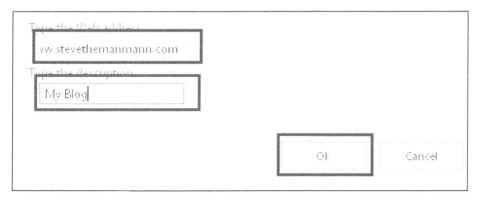

Click OK.

The new link is added to the Top Link Bar:

### Saving Your Changes

When using the Site Settings method of modifying the Top Link Bar, your changes are saved as you make them. Click on the team site link to return to your team site or click on the Site Settings link to return to Site Settings:

# Quick Launch - Edit in Place

The Quick Launch is the navigation located on the left-hand side of your site:

You may modify the Quick Launch links by clicking the EDIT LINKS button:

This places the Quick Launch into edit mode:

## *Removing a Link*

You may easily remove a link by clicking on the X next to it:

## *Reordering Links*

You may easily change the order by selecting a link and dragging it around the Quick Launch:

## Editing Links

While the Quick Launch is in edit mode, if you click on the name of one of the links, you can quickly modify the text:

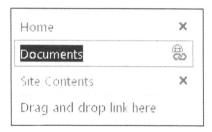

Enter new text and press the Enter key on the keyboard:

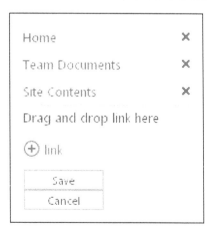

If you wish to edit both the display and the URL, click on the Edit Link button while editing the text:

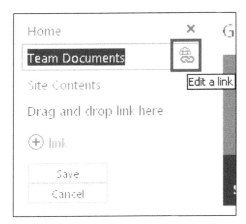

The Edit Link dialog appears:

You may modify the Text to display and the Address of the link. Click OK when finished.

## *Adding a New Link*

To add a new link to the Quick Launch, click on the add link button:

The Add a link dialog appears:

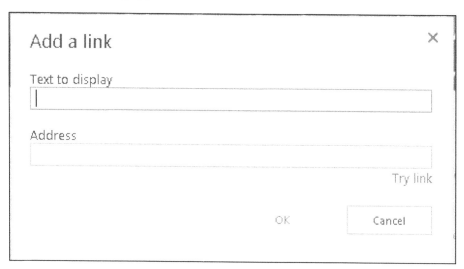

Enter the Text that should be displayed for the link along with an Address.

The address can be an internal SharePoint URL or any external web site:

Click OK.

The new link is added to the Quick Launch:

## Saving Your Changes

Once you have completed the Quick Launch modifications, click the Save button to save the changes and exit out of edit mode:

The changes are saved:

# Quick Launch - Site Settings

You may also modify the Quick Launch using the Site Settings. From the Settings menu, select Site settings:

Under Look and Feel, click on the Quick Launch link:

The Quick Launch page appears:

## *Removing a Link*

To remove a link, click on the Edit button next to the link you wish to delete:

The Edit Navigation Link page appears.

Click on the Delete button to remove the link:

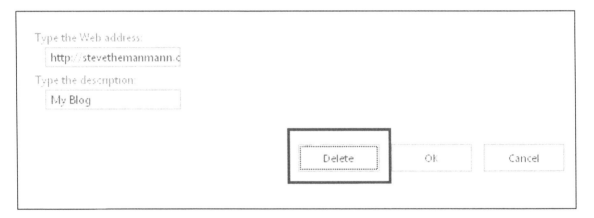

A confirmation message appears:

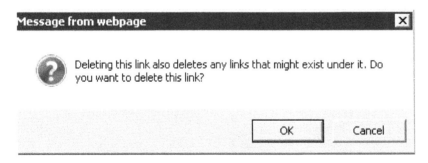

Click OK.

The link is removed:

New Navigation Link | New Heading | Change Order

Home

Team Documents

Site Contents

### Reordering Links

To change the order of the links click on the Change Order button:

The Change Order page appears:

Use the drop-downs to change the order of the links:

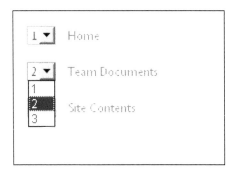

The links are reordered in place:

Click OK to save the ordering changes:

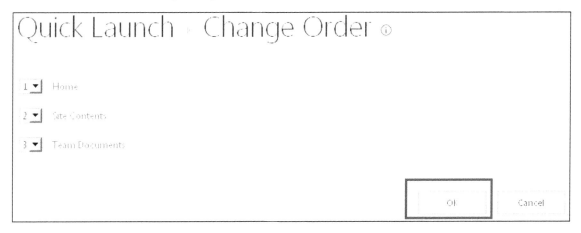

The new order is applied:

## *Editing Links*

To edit an existing link, click on the Edit icon next to the link you wish to modify:

The Edit Navigation Link page appears:

Here you may only modify the description:

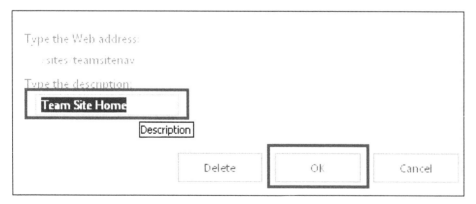

Click OK.

The modification is saved:

New Navigation Link | New Heading | Change Order

Team Site Home

Team Documents

Site Contents

### *Adding a New Link - Heading*

The Quick Launch may contain main links but also have sub-links under the main links. The main links are called Headings.

To create a new Heading link, click on the New Heading button:

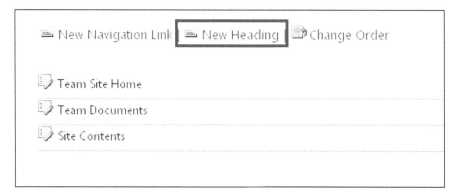

The New Heading page appears:

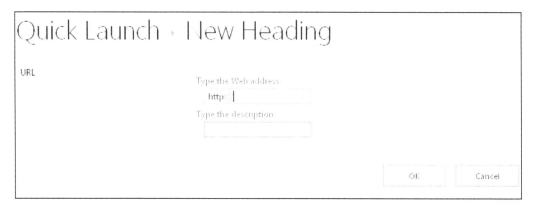

Enter an internal or external web address along with the description:

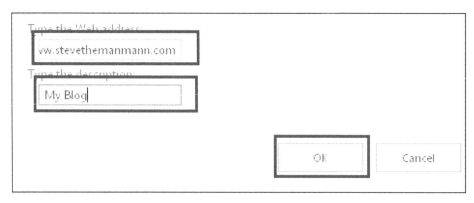

Click OK.

The new heading is added to the Quick Launch:

📄 New Navigation Link | 📄 New Heading | 📋 Change Order

📝 Team Site Home

📝 Team Documents

📝 My Blog

📝 Site Contents

### Adding a New Link - Navigation Link

When you add a new navigation link the link appears under one of the existing headings. Click on the New Navigation Link button:

The New Navigation Link page appears:

Enter an internal or external web address along with the description:

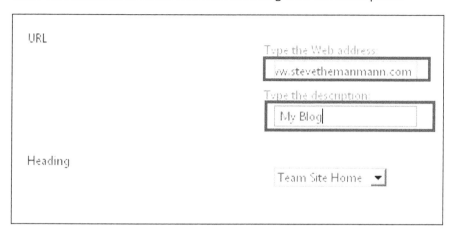

Select which Heading this new link should appear under:

Click OK:

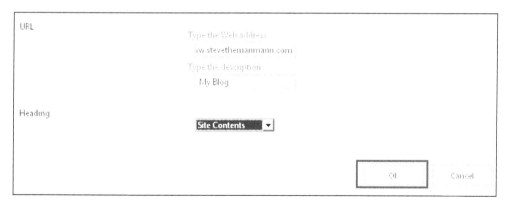

The new link is added to the Quick Launch under the heading selected:

## *Saving Your Changes*

When using the Site Settings method of modifying the Quick Launch, your changes are saved as you make them. Click on the team site link to return to your team site or click on the Site Settings link to return to Site Settings:

## Navigation Settings of Subsites

The original subsites were created with the default settings which means that any navigation is not inherited from the parent site. The parent site in this case is the Team Site site collection. You may inherit the Top Link Bar from your main site by modifying the settings on each subsite.

Navigate to one of your subsites:

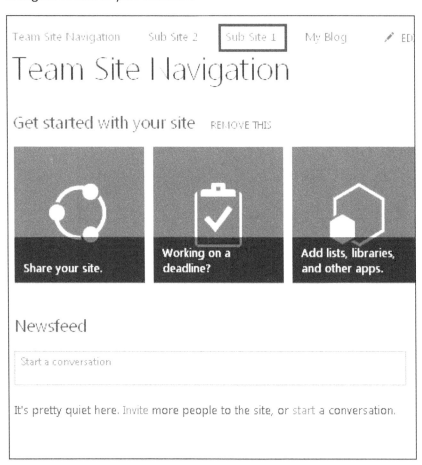

Notice that the Quick Launch and the Top Link Bar have their own settings on the subsite:

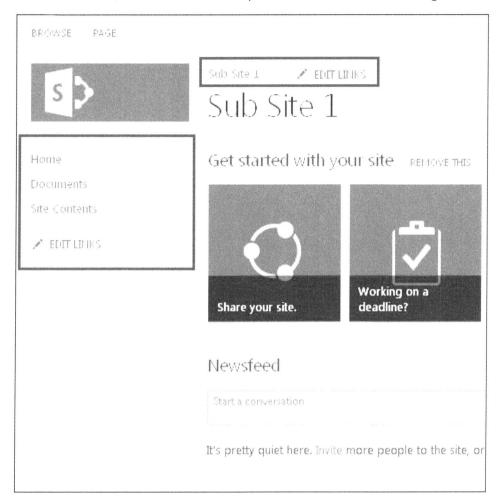

The modifications that were performed on the main site collection (Team Site) do not flow through to the subsites. Since the Quick Launch is based on the current site structure and contents, the Quick Launch cannot be inherited from the main site.

To make sure that at least the Top Link Bar of the subsite looks like the main site collection Top Link Bar, select Site Settings from the Settings menu on your subsite:

Under Look and Feel, click on the Top Link Bar link:

The Top Link Bar page appears:

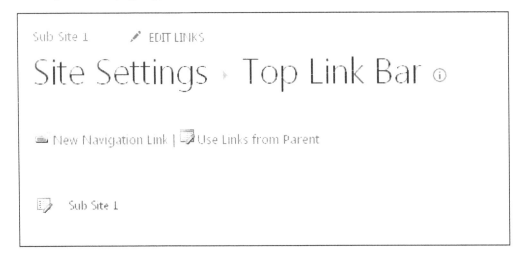

Click on the Use Links from Parent button:

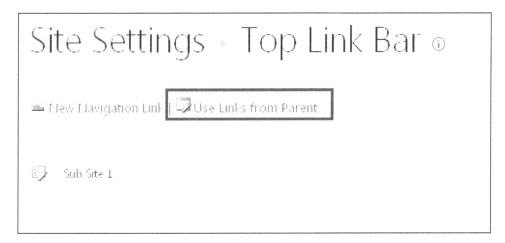

A confirmation message appears:

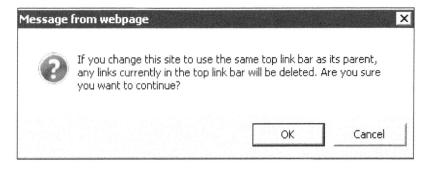

Click OK.

The subsite is now inheriting the Top Link Bar from the main site collection:

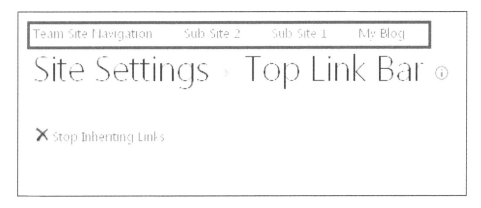

## About the Author

Steve Mann was born and raised in Philadelphia, Pennsylvania, where he still resides. He is an Enterprise Application Engineer for Morgan Lewis and has over 20 years of professional experience. He has authored and co-authored several books related to collaboration technology. Steve graduated Drexel University in 1993.

Steve's blog site can be found at: www.SteveTheManMann.com

Follow Steve on Twitter @stevethemanmann

www.ingramcontent.com/pod-product-compliance
Lightning Source LLC
Chambersburg PA
CBHW060508060326
40689CB00020B/4681